The   Revolver

E.EVANS.Sc

Robt. Adams

POSITION OF THE PISTOL IN LOADING.

MR. ADAMS LOADING THE REVOLVER OF H.R.H. THE PRINCE CONSORT.

THE REVOLVER:

ITS

DESCRIPTION, MANAGEMENT, AND USE;

WITH

𝔥𝔦𝔫𝔱𝔰 𝔬𝔫 𝔯𝔦𝔣𝔩𝔢 𝔠𝔩𝔲𝔟𝔰

AND

THE DEFENCE OF THE COUNTRY.

BY

PATRICK EDWARD DOVE,

ARMS AND ARMOUR PRESS

Published by ARMS AND ARMOUR PRESS
Lionel Leventhal Limited
Trade Distribution: 16 Pembridge Road, London, W.11.

First edition 1858

© Arms and Armour Press, 1968

SBN 85368 160 0

The Publishers are pleased to acknowledge the co-operation of the Borough Librarian of the London Borough of Lewisham in making possible this facsimile edition.

Printed in Great Britain

ILLUSTRATIONS.

From Photographs taken at Beard's by Mr. W. S. Scott, and engraved on Wood by Mr. Edmund Evans.

PRELIMINARY.

VISITING London in the summer of 1857, with the intention—though not altogether for the purpose—of making myself acquainted with the new method of manufacturing fire-arms by machinery, I called, as a matter of course, on Mr. Robert Adams, inventor and patentee of "Adams's Revolver." Mr. Adams freely laid open to me the factory of the London Armoury Company, of which he is Manager, and with the utmost liberality afforded such information as I required. I paid many visits to the factory, and familiarised myself with the processes which Mr. Adams has introduced. The manufacture of Revolvers being comparatively a recent addition to the fire-arm trade of the country, I went narrowly into its details—ascertained the markets for which the pistols were intended, the number produced per week, the wages of the workmen, the cost of production, the mode of distribution, &c., and speculated freely with Mr. Adams

regarding the changes that are looming in the
future of the gun-trade—changes that must neces-
sarily arise out of the substitution of machinery for
hand labour. By so doing, I at least opened up
the way for further inquiries into this branch of
our national industry.

I also visited the Rifle Factory at Enfield, and
admired the perfection of its mechanical results.
Whatever may be said by the defenders of the old
system of fitting the various pieces of a rifled
musket *by hand*, it is unquestionable that the
muskets now made at Enfield are turned out in a
manner with which no human hand, under any
amount of skill or practice, could possibly compete.
The work is so accurate and so sound that there
can be no hesitation in pronouncing the Enfield
rifle to be the best weapon that ever was placed in
the hand of the infantry soldier. I do not like its
bullet, nor do I believe that any cupped bullet has
ever been made to shoot as well as a solid bullet.
But even on this point there is latitude for a
difference of opinion, because the Enfield bullet
being intended for military purposes alone must
combine the military requirements of great power
and easy loading; and therefore an objection " that
some of the bullets go astray" must be judged by
the military standard and not by the standard of
the sportsman or the target-shooter. But as
regards the musket, there can scarcely be a difference of opinion. It is marvellously good. The

establishment may or may not have been a costly
one ; with that part of the matter I have no concern. I look only at the artistic production—at the
weapon as a weapon—as a rifle made with strict
accuracy and consummate adaptation of part to
part ; and it does not admit of question that the
machine-made gun is incomparably superior to
anything that has ever been made by hand. Excellent guns for service may be, and are, made by
hand—that I do not deny—but when the quality of
the work is impartially surveyed by the educated
eye, there is a sharpness and precision, and an
almost invisible fitting of part to part which render
comparison out of the question. And this advantage of strict accuracy, although it may be of little
moment to the individual soldier using the musket,
becomes a great national consideration when a
whole army has to be supplied, and when the
manufacture can be conducted on the principle of
interchangeability—namely, that any part of any
musket will fit the parts of another musket equally
well ; so that in the manufacture it is not requisite
to make *muskets* and to store *muskets*, but only to
make a complete supply of *parts*, for any lock will fit
any stock, and *vice versâ*. The real value of the principle is not so much seen in the field as in the manufacture, which secures the perfect accuracy of every
single weapon at the cheapest rate and in the simplest manner. Hitherto the process may have been
an expensive one, on account of the machinery being

altogether novel, and the men only acquiring the skill of using the machines to the best advantage; but when the article is once produced, the next step, of course, is to produce it as cheaply as possible—that is, by the shortest and simplest processes; but with that part of the matter I have no concern: I am looking at arms as arms, and not as merchandise.

The circumstance that the Rifle should have been known almost from the period of the invention of fire-arms, and that only now, within the last few years, it should have been constructed in a form to become the true weapon of the infantry soldier, naturally led me to speculate on the probability of a similar fate attending the Revolver. I arrived at the conclusion that the genuine merits of the Revolver were comparatively unknown and un-appreciated. Notwithstanding all that has been said and written on the subject, I am thoroughly convinced that even gunmakers scarcely know the real qualities of the revolver-pistols. They sell them, and that is sufficient for their purpose. I therefore stated to Mr. Adams that I would throw my notes together in the form of a pamphlet if he would have his portrait taken in the proper attitude for loading the pistol. He hesitated for a con-siderable time, not wishing for the prominence con-ferred by the photographer and engraver. He had never courted publicity, and thought that as the officers appointed by the War Department to examine into the merits of the various Revolvers had pronounced in favour of his patent, their decision ought to be sufficient for the public. To this I demurred, and said, in plain words, " That decision is sufficient to establish the quality of the arm in its military capacity and reputation ; but the public, as well as the army, requires to know something about Revolvers, therefore have your portrait taken, to show how the pistol should be held in loading, and I will sketch out a few observations, which you shall see when published, but not before."

At this time the news arrived of the Indian mutiny, and all eyes were turned to India. Letter after letter spoke of *revolvers*. Lieut. Kutznow, who received the thanks of the Governor-General, " mourned that he had not had a couple of revolvers ;" another officer " could have shot a good many of them if he had had a revolver ;" another thanked his friends at home for the revolver they had sent him (a Colt, I believe), and stated " that he could get £50 for it," so highly was the weapon esteemed—there being only two at the station. Another says, " I crept behind a bush, and never felt more grateful for a revolver." Another, " I am dreadfully in want of a revolver ; no man is safe here without one. All those that were disposable in the country have been bought up. The Government at home would confer a great boon upon those who have not revolvers if they were to sanction an issue of them."

This Indian mutiny decided the hesitation of Mr. Adams. A man's modesty may be allowed to stand in the way of his personal interest, but not in the way of his public duty. I urged on Mr. Adams the imperative duty of bringing his weapon prominently forward as the very thing that was wanted under the peculiarities of this most terrible catastrophe. If Revolvers had been plentiful in India, many a gallant life might have been saved —ay, and what is more, the ladies and the poor little children might have escaped—some, at least —the tortures and the agony of such deaths as British mothers and British children have never known before, and may God in mercy grant may never know again.*

When the Indian news came home (and was *understood*), I saw the advantages of Revolvers in a light which I confess I had not seen before, namely, that while our own people could be supplied with them, the insurgent troops could not procure them. We had, with a species of military infatuation, given our Enfield rifles to the Sepoys, and consequently had retained in our own hands no weapon superior to that which we had given to the native; a sheer blunder of the most preposterous kind, and

---

* Miss Wheeler, daughter of Sir H. Wheeler, is reported to have shot five of her assailants with a revolver before she fell a victim to the atrocities at Cawnpore. But perhaps this account may have originated in the feat of Lieut. Sanders, 84th Regt., or have been confounded with the story of the younger Miss Wheeler.

probably arising out of a species of military puppy-
ism which would have these conceited Brahmins of
Bengal armed with the best of all possible weapons,
when, in reality, there was no enemy against which
the Enfield rifles could in their hands be employed
except ourselves. A flint musket is quite good
enough for them to do the work of tax-gatherers
and policemen. As to genuine fighting, in the first
place they had nobody to fight with, and on the
frontiers, where fighting might be expected, the
real work must always fall upon the British troops
in the long run. It was therefore an error of the
most serious kind to give these cockatoo Brahmins
of Bengal the Enfield rifle, and the sooner the error
is repaired the better. But what is the next best
thing to do? evidently to send out to India a large
supply of this new weapon—the Revolver—that all
India may know that a new weapon, not attainable
by the natives, has arrived by thousands—a weapon
which can shoot five men in five seconds, and which
can be carried in the pocket, the belt, or the holster
by pairs. Let India know that fact, and let all
Europeans in India make a point of procuring
Revolvers and exhibiting them as need may be, and
we should soon see the impression in the fears of
the population. If Colt's pistol (a good weapon
for certain purposes, but inferior to Adams's for
military work) has had the effect of putting down
the Indian wars and Indian incursions in the
frontier states of the Union, surely it could not be

unreasonable to anticipate that a similar effect would be produced in India, and that the presence of the Revolver universally in the hands of the Europeans would tend immensely to the security of British rule. Under this impression I wrote a letter to the *Times* on the subject; but even an editor of the *Times* cannot be expected to know everything, and the letter appears to have been trundled into the Balaam box. I mention this, however, for the purpose of protesting that the subject has not been overlooked *beforehand*, and has been brought before the notice of the *Times—beforehand*. After the Crimean disasters, it looked marvellously clever to discourse upon picks that would not pick, and shovels that would not dig, because then the realised fact was a great conspicuous fact, and the criticism was carried along on the back of the fact, like a magpie on the top of a ram. It might suit the *Times* to discourse on the useless picks and shovels after the fact, but why not do so *before?* True—a caution beforehand does not and cannot look so grand as an exposure afterwards; but who cares for that, when difficulty surrounds the State, and good can be done by speaking out, be the caution, or be it not, estimated as worthy or as worthless? Any person taking the trouble could have found out *beforehand* that the picks would not pick, and that the shovels would not dig, either by giving them a day's work on Blackheath, or by ascertaining that the contracts were taken below manufacturers' prices, by speculators who had a rotten material made purposely, as bad as it could be made, so as to allow themselves a profit. This could have been found out *beforehand*, and good picks and shovels could have been bought without difficulty. And so in this matter of the Revolver for India. It may look at present only a mere suggestion; but if the news comes home from India that hundreds of lives could have been saved *by revolvers*—as most certainly must have been the case whether the announcement may or may not be put in those words—then we may expect whole rivers of criticism, splendidly written, but *too late*.

In this crisis, therefore, none need hesitate to bring before the attention of the Government and of the country the imperative necessity of sending Revolvers to India; of arming the cavalry and the engineers with them, the artillery under certain circumstances, and even a certain number of men in each regiment of European foot. Sooner or later our men *must* come to close quarters with the Sepoys, and the revolver is the very best of all fire-arms for close work.

And again, it is a perfectly well-known fact all over the world, that half-civilised people are afraid of a superior weapon which they do not understand. When cannon were first introduced, they did more damage by their reputation than by their fire. It has always been the same with fire-arms used against savages. Savages do not like to be shot at.

It would be the same in India. The Enfield rifle, if carefully kept from the native troops, and only shown to them in its effects, its long range and great accuracy of fire would have impressed them deeply with a sense of their inferior chance in a contest with the British. We gave them the Enfield rifle, and thereby did wrong. Let us now turn the chances once more in our own favour by giving our troops the Revolver. All India would soon know the fact, and all the natives, without exception, would feel themselves beaten, or placed in almost a hopeless position by the consciousness that they would have to encounter men who could annihilate them if ever they came within reach. The moral impression on India would be the gain of half an army. The nation, as a collection of half-civilised tribes (for there is no Indian nation, and no Indian nationality), would effectually succumb, and the insurgents, as a body of armed traitors, could be hunted down at leisure all the more easily when the general inhabitants were cowed, and when the mutineers found that the success of their insurrection had been rendered utterly hopeless. All future disturbance would be incomparably more dangerous to them than it had ever been before, and consequently the British occupation of India would be placed on a more secure basis, and the whole of the vast dominion could be brought more immediately and directly under the government of the British crown.

The present pamphlet is therefore written for the purpose of calling attention to the subject of Revolvers, and also, quite explicitly and avowedly, for the purpose of pointing out more particularly than has hitherto been done in print, the peculiarities of Mr. Adams's pistol. After careful examination, I feel satisfied that this pistol is decidedly the best that has hitherto appeared in this country ; that it combines the greatest number of advantages, and is the most efficient for service. It may be said that this is the opinion of a friend and partisan. Be it so. I am content that even that charge should be made by the ignorant or the interested. Those who understand the real question in hand, and the paramount importance of a good weapon in time of need, will not be numbered among the objectors. If criticism be applied to books, pictures, and parliamentary proceedings, I see no reason why criticism should not also be applied to arms. The criticism may stand for as much as it is worth.

P. E. D.

THE REVOLVER.

THE Rifle and the Revolver are nearly as old as the invention of fire-arms. No one knows who invented them, where they were first introduced, nor even to what country they originally belong. They are now the best and most efficient of all weapons, yet for centuries they lay slumbering in the old store-houses of arms, or, where they appeared, it was in such guise and garb that their splendid capabilities were altogether overlooked or ignorantly sneered at. In the Tower of London there is a primitive old Revolver that dates most likely as far back as the Tudors; and, if I mistake not, I have seen a similar one, perhaps not quite so old but on the same principle, in the Museum of Darmstadt. It is at all events certain that Revolvers were made several centuries ago, and that they have only recently come into common use. Military officers with all their professional knowledge, and gun-makers with all their practical skill, had overlooked the fact that the Tower of London contained a weapon of sterling excellence, which, if properly turned to account, might have made any man's fortune and wonderfully increased the martial strength of the country. So much for practical men, even in the midst of wars which might have sharpened the wits of the nation. But no—the Revolver was unheeded, and there it stands in its rack to this day as a proof how merit may be overlooked until somebody begins to blow its trumpet. It was the same with the Rifle, or nearly so. The Rifle, though not as old as the hills, is so old that nobody knows its parentage. Whoever invented it must have been a man of genius, a man of far sight into the world of science, a man of sound logic who reasoned boldly, and did not shrink from his conclusions, a man who had his head screwed on the right way, a man who did not stumble on a truth by chance but wrested it from nature by reason, an A 1 man in the books of all generations henceforth —till people give up shooting each other with rifles. The barometer or the compensating pendulum are not finer deductions than that of the twisted groove. There is nothing in mechanics superior to it. It is a genuine insight into the construction of our terrestrial system—nay, for that matter, even of our celestial—for the planets themselves are rifled, and that is the reason they perform so well. Were the planets not rifled the whole solar system would go incontinently to smash ; and the first man who made a rifle was a genius of the truest insight, who had

the eye of a Newton to see into the principles of
nature.   He is forgotten-- peace be to his ashes !—
for that is the way the world sometimes deals with
merit of the highest order.

But the Rifle, after scraping through a species
of curiosity-shop existence, and being practically
bungled as much as it was possible to bungle a great
invention, came at last to be recognised as something
more than a mere toy or ingenious trifle.   The game
of America—the deer, turkeys, coons, bears, squirrels
and Indians—called the small-bored rifle into
excellent practice.   The game was exactly the thing
for the rifle, and the rifle was exactly the thing for
the game.   As the rifles increased, the game
diminished, and consequently the rifles were made
better and better, till now, the real American rifle of
the first class—small bore, 75 to the pound, cast
steel barrel and telescope sight—is about as near
perfection as an English race-horse or a Damascus
sword-blade.   But it is a *hunting* rifle not a *war*
rifle, except, indeed, in a thickly-wooded country
where long range and general field engagements are
not the order of the day.   America showed at least
what could be done with the small bore, and, in so
doing, contributed her natural share to the improvement of the weapon.

Germany, again, had good, quiet, inoffensive rifles,
(like her soldiers)—rifles of moderate calibre, moderate length, moderate charge, and of very fair
performance at very moderate distances.

France understood the Rifle in no possible way whatever. The Frenchman's head is not screwed on the right way for mechanics. His *carabine à balle forcée* was frequently a foolish perpetration. He had even occasionally the grooves *straight.* He did not understand the " music of the spheres," and had never reflected on the fact that the planets were rifled.

The English rifle, on the other hand, was John Bull all over. He would have it *strong*—a big bore, a stock like a tree, a steel ramrod, and everything else in proportion. Such was John's idea of a rifle. A thing that would blow a hole right through an elephant and crack the skull of a tiger as easy as an egg-shell—that was the article for John's money. And if it only *looked* formidable John was satisfied, for small understanding had he of the matter until of late years. The two-grooved Brunswick rifle, with a banded spherical ball and a turn in 2 feet 6 inches, was one of John's latest ideas before the invasion of the new system which has wiped out all remembrance of the old. The Rifle is now a war-weapon of terrific power and precision ; yet ten years ago there were very few indeed—officers, amateurs, or gunmakers—who had the slightest conception of what a rifle could really be made to do. Foremost of the objectors to the Rifle, and first in favour of old Brown Bess, was His Grace Field Marshal the Duke of Wellington, who " couldn't a bear 'em." And so, perhaps, if Nelson were to come back again

his first anathema would be on the tea-kettles that
we now call ships.   But no; Nelson was too great a
man for prejudices against the instruments of war
(though in his younger days he could not stand the
epaulettes), a far truer Englishman than Field Marshal the Duke of Wellington—the greatest warrior-
Englishman, in fact, since the days of little
Admiral Blake—five feet six—who in nine years of
his seaman's life swept the ocean so completely of
the foes of his country, that when he went his way
there was not a single flag afloat to face the red St.
George of England.

The Rifle, then, within the last few years has come
into practical and purposelike employment.   It is
now the weapon of our infantry, and with it they
must win our battles.   But it is a weapon centuries
old, and only now adapted to the full requirements
of the service.   It had a long hill to climb before
its true merits were known or recognised—a long
period of neglect and a whole host of absurd prejudices to overcome.

The same may be true of the Revolver.   It is
apparently as old, perhaps older, than the rifle; yet
only recently has it gained a fair footing; and even
now it is served out in driblets, as the rifle was
once.   The Rifle and the Revolver are, in fact, the
true arms of the infantry soldier.   The two should
go together—the Rifle for the long range and the
bayonet rush—the Revolver for the assault, the
melée, and the surprise.   And above all, the cavalry

soldier ought to have it. He is put on a horse to give him quickness of action, and he is encumbered with a barbarous carbine which impedes all his movements and which he very properly cuts away whenever he has serious work to perform with the sword.* Now instead of this carbine, why not give him a revolver, which he can use with one hand, or even two revolvers, one in each holster? and then, whenever he charges he carries with him the best weapon for the skirmish or the close fight. The thing would be advantageous every way (except that Routine, and Things as they are, might have a little trouble in the first instance), and the cavalry soldier would be a more confident man as well as incomparably a more powerful man in the field. If it came to shooting, he would whip out his pistol with the reflection that "two can play at that ;" and if it came to sabreing, he would sabre none the worse because he had first emptied a few saddles, and seen a few of the enemy on the ground by the aid of his left-hand revolver. Give the soldier confidence in his arms and you give him half the victory, and to give him confidence give him—say I, for one—a well-made and efficient revolver. It seems, in fact, a sort of infatuation on the part of the Government not to be sending out thousands of revolvers to India at the present time, and an infatuation on the

* A letter I saw yesterday, from an officer before Delhi, deplores "that the weight of the carabineers and their accoutrements render them almost useless."—*Times*.

C

part of the country to allow the neglect—for the country has a right to know that every possible advantage which could be given to our forces has actually been supplied to them. As to the expense —the expense is a matter of moonshine. The country would in six hours' notice authorise the purchase of every revolver in the known world, if that purchase would aid in the renewed subjugation of India, and in the greater security of the British who are there.

Of this I feel confident, from the study I have made of arms, that the revolver, at the present time, is in much the same position as the rifle was a few years since. Its genuine qualities and adaptation for universal service are unknown or overlooked. It must come into the service eventually, and now is the best of all times to rush it on as fast as machines and men can be got to make it. Instead of being made by dozens or by hundreds, it should be made by thousands, till there is a revolver almost for every man on service—a store here and a store there— abundance everywhere; till the whole world knows that the whole of the British army is fully revol- vered, a knowledge that would do troublesome neighbours a world of good, and make them think many more times than twice before they attempted improper liberties with the British nation. Our militia at home ought to have revolvers as well as rifles : and if the governing authorities would fairly encourage the use of the rifle as a great national sport

—as a substitute for the old archery sports of the bygone times of England—and have rifle clubs of decent men in every parish and village, town and county, and give public prizes, and have the whole under proper management and control, and add the revolver to the rifle, and let matches be shot everywhere with both weapons, the whole world itself could not touch our island security. As Oliver Cromwell somewhat irreverently said, "If Frenchman, Pope, Spaniard, and devil, and all were to combine," they could not touch us—they might as well walk into a volcano.

That is what I mean by recommending Mr. Adams's Revolver to the pressing notice of all concerned in the security and welfare of Britain, and in the success of the British arms. Commercially, Mr. Adams needs no recommendation from any one. But although fortune may not have withheld her favours, his weapon requires to be better and more widely known, and its peculiarities more distinctly pointed out. I proceed, therefore, to its description.

PARTS OF THE REVOLVER.

THE parts of the Revolver are :—
      1. The Frame.
      2. The Cylinder.
      3. The Action.
      4. The Lever Rod.
      5. The Furniture.
      6. The Stock.

THE FRAME.

The Frame, which includes the barrel of the pistol, is made of a single piece of the best quality of iron that can be procured, known as Marshall's iron. It is not welded, but cut out of the solid. It has no joint in it of any kind, but is *one piece of iron.* The angles are therefore as secure as the strength of the metal can make them ; and the frame being *centred* once for all, is worked true in all the after processes of boring, rifling, and fitting.

To give an idea of the processes through which the parts of a pistol are carried in the course of

CYLINDER. FRAME WITH STOCK, ETC.
PRINCE ALBERT'S REVOLVER.

manufacture, we may take the frame as an instance.   The frame is first forged to very nearly the
outward shape which it is to retain.   It is then a
solid piece of iron, with a thick block at one end
and the barrel at the other.   It is then centred,
that is, a point at each end is marked and struck as
the centre of future operations.   The centre keeps
everything true.   It is then planed on the outside.
It is then slotted ; that is, the place for the cylinder
is cut out of the solid block.   It is then bored and
rifled, then filed up and fitted.   It then receives the
action (lock, &c.) ; is then stocked and proved ; has
the bolt and lever-rod fitted ; is polished, engraved,
blued, screwed together, and then shot.

THE CYLINDER.

The Cylinder is also made of Marshall's iron, or
of steel.   If of the former, it is case-hardened.
The cylinder is bored with five chambers, a number
abundantly sufficient for all the ordinary purposes
of use.   It must never be forgotten that the design-
ing of a pattern fire-arm is a question of the compensation of advantages.   On rare occasions it
might be advantageous to have six, eight, or ten
chambers : more often it would be found that three
or four were all that were required.   It is necessary,
therefore, to select out of all the numbers that
which is found practically to combine the fullest
measure of efficiency with the greatest amount of

convenience.   An odd number is required in an
Adams's pistol, on account of the spur of the trigger, which comes forward when the trigger is drawn
back, and fixes the cylinder at the moment of discharge.   By pulling the trigger and looking at the
mechanism of rotation you will observe, that when
the cylinder comes to its proper place it is held firm
by a projection which prevents the cylinder from
revolving further.   With an even number, that
projection would face the open space where the
cones are placed.   In an Adams's pistol the nipples
or cones are screwed in.   In some of Colt's pistols
the nipples are made of the solid metal, an arrangement which prevents the fitting of a new cone in
case of fracture or injury.   The central hole, through
which the pin passes, is bored so as to make the
cylinder touch the pin only at the two extremities,
thereby lessening the friction.   At the back of the
cylinder is the ratchet, to give the revolving mo-
tion to the cylinder when acted on by the project-
ing lever of the trigger action, called, technically, the
lifter.   The cylinder, when finished, is case-hardened.
The ratchet is made of steel.

THE ACTION.

The Action consists of :—
A. The main spring.
B. The swivel.
C. The hammer.
D. The short scear.

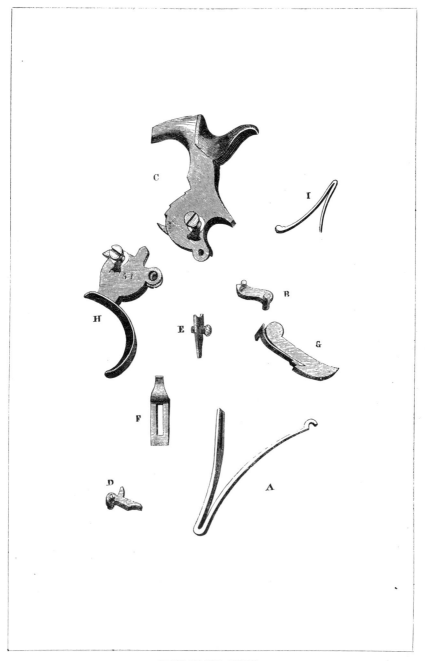

PARTS OF THE ACTION.

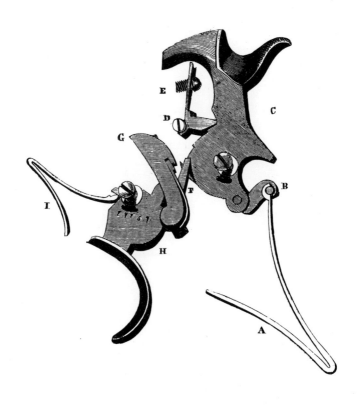

THE ACTION IN POSITION.

E. The short scear spring.

F. The long scear.

G. The lifter, with the spring which works both lifter and long scear.

H. The trigger.

I. The trigger spring.

The four screws or pins—hammer pin, trigger pin, short scear pin, and short scear spring pin.

The mode of action may be seen by looking at the engraving. Thus—

When the trigger is pulled the long scear pushes up the hammer, and the lifter pushes round the ratchet of the cylinder. As the hammer goes up, its circular portion, called *the belly*, pushes the long scear forward, so that it goes out of the notch, and the hammer falls on the nipple or cone. When the pistol is cocked by pulling back the hammer, the short scear goes into the full bend notch, and the long scear is pulled up close to the short scear by the hook on the hammer, which by this action draws back the trigger. When the trigger is then pulled, the long scear pushes the short scear out of the notch, and the hammer falls.

After one shot has been fired the finger must be slackened so as to allow the trigger to go forward to its original place, which it does by the action of I, the trigger spring.

This lock is not apparently simple, but it has the great merit of working well for almost any number of shots, and does not get out of order. I believe a thousand shots have been fired with the same pistol without difficulty; but I cannot certify to the fact, not having been present. But I have taken a pistol from the store—any one out of a hundred—and with Mr. John Adams, have shot it till we were tired—certainly above three hundred shots; and, with the exception that the pistol got a little dirty from the burnt powder, there was no appearance of its being less efficient at the end of the trial than at the beginning. The lock is excellent: to that fact I can safely certify.

THE ADVANTAGES OF ADAMS'S PISTOL.

The essential quality of a rifle is that it shall shoot accurately. *Accuracy* is the first requisite—to be combined, of course, with as much power, convenience, and rapidity of action as can be secured without sacrificing accuracy of performance. With the pistol it is different. *Rapidity of action* is the first quality of a pistol, to be combined, of course, with as much accuracy and range as can be secured without sacrificing rapidity. We should not value a rifle that could shoot one or two more shots in a minute if we could not depend upon the accuracy of its fire; neither should we value a pistol that could shoot very accurately at two or three hundred yards if we were compelled to spend much time and care in its adjustment every time it was fired. A pistol being required for short ranges and rapid perform-

ance, that pistol is the best which does its work
most rapidly and with the fewest actions of the
arm or fingers, provided it shoots with equal accuracy and power.   The whole theory of the manufacture of arms is that of a compensation of advantages;
and the best arm is the one in which the advantages are most judiciously combined according to
the nature of the weapon.   In this respect Mr.
Adams's pistol excels all others that have hitherto
been made. It shoots with *one* action. That, in
fact, is the first requisite of a good military pistol—
namely, that it can be seized with one hand, right
or left, and fired in a moment with a single draw of
the trigger finger.   To pull up the hammer, as in
Colt's, is a superfluous and most disadvantageous
drawback; while a double action, as in Tranter's, is a
similar error, as one cannot be expected to play the
fiddle on a pistol when in action.   But it is said
that a pistol is more dangerous when it can be fired
by a draw of the finger.   Exactly; and that is the
very reason that it is the best.   The sharpest razor
is the most dangerous for children or persons who
do not know how to use it.   But the sharpest razor
is the best because it is the sharpest.   And so it is
with Adams's pistol.   The very quality which
makes it preeminently good for service is the quality
that makes it dangerous in the hands of boys and
bunglers. A pistol that requires two actions to fire
it is more safe in a house than one that requires
only a single action; one that required three would

be still more safe; and one that would not go off at
all, as sometimes happens with those that have
complex and fanciful notions attached to them,
would be perfectly safe. Adams's pistol is not
constructed for what is absurdly termed safety
(which is procured by *blunting the razor*), but for
action—for the most rapid action that can be
executed with the simplest effort. It is the
elementary pistol, and the best for military service
because it is elementary. To it may be added
half-a-dozen new arrangements, all tending to make
it more safe, and all tending to deprive it of its
elementary character of simplicity, which, in my
estimation, is its peculiar claim to the foremost
rank among revolving arms. I do not say that it
can never be improved, but that its principle is the
best of all, and must be adhered to under all circumstances. But I certainly should depart very far
from my intention were I to say anything in
prejudice of Colonel Colt's weapon, which is a good
pistol for America and for American purposes—
namely, where the pistol requires to be used as half
a rifle with a long aim. Colt's pistol for military
purposes is a mistake; but it is a good pistol for
hunting purposes and for single shots at Indians,
buffaloes, bears, and deer, though even for that
service Adams's is preferable, because the *secona
shot*, which is often of the utmost consequence, can
be given at once without taking down the pistol
or going off the aim. In fact, the best way to use

a Colt in a hurry is to fix up the trigger altogether and fire by snapping the hammer, in which case it becomes an inferior form of an Adams. Adams's pistol, like a Colt, can be fired from the full cock, a part of the action which was introduced by an officer in the army; but I certainly do not consider it an improvement. The half bend is a good, useful, and necessary stop; but the full bend is not required, as the pistol fires more pleasantly with its own proper sliding draw than out of the full bend notch. However, some may prefer to cock the pistol when firing at a mark, and the pistol has the action, if required; but, for my own part, I think it unnecessary.

In the construction of Adams's pistol there is an advantage, which many would overlook, and even gunmakers are scarcely aware of it. It is that the action of the hammer and the revolving action are disconnected. Pull back the trigger as if you had just fired, and then pull up the hammer as if the hammer had been blown up by the force of the escape from the cone, and you will observe that you have not rotated the cylinder nor set the revolving parts in action. Whenever a pistol is fired, there is, of course, a certain springing back of the hammer, and this, constantly repeated, would be apt to throw the works out of order if the hammer and mainspring (as in Colt's) were to affect the rotation of the cylinder. In an Adams's pistol the hammer and mainspring are isolated, and the hammer may be driven back as violently as possible without affecting any part of the works except the spring. And this arrangement contributes greatly to the *durability* of the pistol. It does not get out of order, which is the great drawback of other pistols.

Another advantage of Adams's pistol is that it does not shoot *all round*. When one barrel is fired it does not discharge the others; and this is the result of leaving the chambers and the nipples fully open, so that the inflamed gas is not confined and driven into the other chambers or on the other nipples. It would be more convenient, perhaps, in case of rain to have a cover over the nipples; but the disadvantage of shooting all round would be a fatal objection. The cover was the great drawback to the first revolver introduced by Mr. Collier.

Thoroughly to satisfy yourself regarding the advantages and disadvantages of the various actions that are applied to revolvers, try the following conclusive experiment. A pistol, be it ever remembered, is intended for rapid work at short distances; therefore, to test the various kinds, try the following plan. Take a revolver in your hand, go to a door, open it suddenly, and snap the pistol at five different objects inside of the door. Try the plan first with the pistol in your right hand, then with the pistol in your left hand, as some doors open with the hinges to the right, and some with the hinges to the left, a circumstance which may make it of the greatest consequence to be able to use the pistol with either hand. I say that the pistol that enables you to shoot at the five objects in the shortest time, with either hand, is the best and most serviceable weapon; and unquestionably it is the single-actioned pistol that goes off with a single draw of one finger. If you are compelled to cock with your thumb, you not only lose time and are compelled to take the pistol down, but, from pulling both finger and thumb at once, you will run the risk of firing when you did not intend to fire; and if you are compelled to use your middle finger as well as your fore-finger, you not only lose time and confuse yourself with alternating the draw, but you run the risk of having your middle finger cut off with a sword stroke, supposing that there are swords inside, a circumstance tolerably certain in India at the present time. To speak without reserve, I say, unhesitatingly, that no other advantage—no powerful shooting, or accurate shooting, at *long* distances —could possibly compensate, in my opinion, for the absence of the *single draw*. The single draw is the *sine quâ non* of a perfect pistol; it is the first requisite, compared with which all other qualities are of minor importance.

This point becomes more apparent when we consider the elementary qualities of the various arms— the qualities which require to be combined in certain proportions. I should therefore rank the qualities thus—

For the Rifle.	*For the Pistol.*
1. Accuracy.	1. Rapidity.
2. Power or penetration.	2. Power or penetration.
3. Rapidity.	3. Accuracy.

The Shot Gun.

1. Proper distribution of shot.
2. Rapidity of action.
3. Power of penetration.
4. Accuracy of both barrels.

It is quite possible to make any one of these elementary qualities predominate. We can give a pistol very great power of penetration, if we are so inclined ; so also we can give a rifle great rapidity. But I maintain that all exaggerations of any one quality at the expense of the others, and especially at the expense of the essential quality No. 1, ends in the production of a monstrosity, and not of a serviceable weapon. And such a monstrosity is now being sent to India in the shape of Sharp's carbine, a weapon which, for a cavalry soldier, is, in my humble opinion, about as execrably bad as any weapon that could be designed, except that it has the one good quality of breech-loading, which, if a cavalry soldier must have a carbine, is proper and legitimate. Very long range for a cavalry weapon is about as absurd as it would be to have a shot gun that could kill snipes on the wing at 200 yards—a distance at which they might possibly be killed if they were hit, but at which they certainly never would be hit, except by accident and good luck, once in a week perhaps. Whenever, therefore, you hear of a rifle that will shoot more rapidly, or of a pistol that will shoot further, &c., &c., always ask if the essential quality has not been sacrificed.

MANAGEMENT.

LOADING.

1. BE sure to load your pistol properly, and take pains to do it well on all occasions. The good habit once acquired, may be of vital service in time of need.

2. To load, pull the trigger till the pistol is at half cock.

3. Hold your pistol in your left hand with the muzzle up and the butt against your chest. With your right hand place a cartridge in one of the chambers, turn the cylinder till the ball is under the rod, and force down the charge with the lever. Do the same with the other four chambers, put on the caps, and the pistol is ready for action. If the weapon is not to be used immediately, bolt the cylinder with the bolt at the side, and the pistol is safe.

If you load with loose powder instead of cartridge, be sure that the measure of your pistol flask is filled in the first place, and then properly emptied into the chamber. Put in the ball, and force home as with cartridge.

Nota Bene.—Always be sure that the bullets are well greased.

CHARGE OF POWDER.

For a 38 bore, or largest-sized pistol, five-eighths of a drachm *at least*.

For a 54 bore, or medium-sized pistol, three-eighths of a drachm *at least*.

For a 120 bore, or smallest-sized pistol, three-sixteenths of a drachm *at least*.

HOW TO BURST A REVOLVER.

Put a pinch of powder into one of the chambers, just sufficient to drive the ball into the barrel, but not through it. Fire that charge, and the ball will stick in the barrel. Then fire a full charge, and if the thing has been properly done, the barrel will very likely be found bulged. Fire another full charge, and the barrel will bulge still more; another, and the bulge will still increase; another, and possibly the barrel will be found cracked. It will be observed that *all the balls have remained in the barrel*. This artful way of bursting a pistol is supposed to have been employed at certain trials that shall be nameless.

Nota Bene.—The revolver cannot be burst by an overcharge of powder.

HOW TO PRODUCE ACCIDENTS.

1st. How to be shot yourself. Take a revolver, loaded and unbolted, hold it by the barrel with the

D

muzzle towards you. Hand it to your friend who is unaccustomed to the use of arms. He will very likely grasp it with his finger on the trigger, and shoot you in the left side.

2nd. How to shoot your friend. Take a revolver, loaded and unbolted, place it on your knee, if you are sitting down, hold the muzzle towards him, and begin fiddling with the lock to see how it acts. When you least expect it, the weapon will very likely go off, and you will shoot your friend from the most unpardonable carelessness and folly.

MORAL.

In handling a loaded pistol, make it your invariable rule to handle it vertically; hold the muzzle straight up or down, except when going to fire. Up is the best, for down you may shoot yourself through the foot.

Nota Bene.—A Revolver is no more dangerous than any other pistol.

CLEANING.

1. Be sure to keep your pistol clean.
2. Never take your pistol to pieces. If you begin to tinker your fire-arms about, for the purpose of seeing how they are made, you are eminently likely to put them out of order, or to fail in putting them together again properly. The revolver does not require to be taken to pieces, but only to be cleaned after use.

3. To clean the pistol, therefore,

First—Pull the trigger till the pistol is at half-cock.

Second—Turn the little thumb-screw (technically, the fly-pin) at the side, so as to relieve the cylinder-pin; then draw the cylinder-pin, and remove the cylinder sideways from the body of the pistol.

Third—If you have hot water at hand, plunge the cylinder into it, and wipe it dry with the cleaning-rod and tow or rag; then oil it, both inside and out, with good sweet oil. If you have no hot water at hand, oil alone will clean the cylinder perfectly well; only take care to clear the nipples and to remove all the crust of the burnt powder.

Fourth—Do not put the *barrel* in water, as thereby you might wet or steam the lock, and cause rust; but clean it entirely with oil and tow. Also clean and oil the frame, especially the under part of the upper strap, where the flash takes place. Wipe and oil the hammer and the rest of the metal-work. Put in the cylinder; ram home the cylinder-pin; turn the little thumb-screw; and the pistol is ready for service.

RIFLE CLUBS, AND THE DEFENCE OF THE COUNTRY.

If any one were to affirm that an army invincible for the defence of the country could be raised, supported, and permanently maintained at an expense of 200,000*l.* or 300,000*l.* per annum, we should most likely hear exclamations about Captain Bobadil and Baron Munchausen. I maintain, on the contrary, that the thing is possible, and, if possible, certainly very desirable, considering that steam has partly bridged over the English Channel, and that on the other side of the channel there are some three or four hundred thousand men under arms, who, if they are never to be allowed to fight, might just as well never have been soldiers. Those who suppose that the continental powers are going to disarm because disarming would be particularly convenient to Great Britain while she is engaged with India, must have a large measure of convenient credulity. I apprehend that they have not made themselves particularly well acquainted with the true nature of *Tour-lou-rou.* There is nothing in this nether world that that whole nation would like so well as to humble the pride of *perfide Albion.* " *Et puis nous prendrons Gibraltère, comme nous avons pris Sebastopol.*"

When the *Times* tells us that the continent of Europe is all as mild as milk, and that no possible danger is to be anticipated from our excellent friends, allies, and sympathisers, it is quite natural for the country to suppose that the *Times*—whose especial vocation it is to deal in wholesale politics—does not venture the assertion without reason. Most profoundly must we all hope that the anticipation is correct. At the same time, there are certain little elements of scepticism which intrude themselves on the minds and memories of those of weaker faith. " Better be sure than be sorry," says the proverb ; and it might probably be as well for Great Britain to make herself perfectly safe—which, of course, would afford the liveliest satisfaction to our continental friends and sympathisers. That we should be distressed with unreasonable and preposterous fears must of course be distressing to their sympathetic dispositions ; and the sooner they see us restored to our accustomed strength and indifference, the sooner will they be able to cease all speculations regarding the state of our insular health and prosperity.

In nine years from this present month of September, it will be eight centuries since Duke William of Normandy came over with his knights and

founded the Norman dynasty of England. Eight
centuries form rather a considerable period in the
history of European politics; and if the past be the
parent of the present and the future, and can indicate
to us the probable features of the unborn times, we
may be excused for looking back on those eight
centuries with a certain amount of curiosity as to
the indications they present. We are told that we
are to have no more wars with the Continent; that
we have all grown so wise and so good that we can
do without fighting; and that the past generations
of Britons and Frenchmen were only deluded and
stupid people, who really did not understand their
own interests. Very likely!

But what say the eight centuries? Out of all
that long period, how much has been war and how
much has been peace? How many of the British
or the English monarchs ascended the throne and
went to their royal graves without shedding the
blood of the continentals? If we count them over,
there is an inconvenient name of something called a
battle (and, thanks to our stupid forefathers, who
did not understand their own interests, the battle
was in most cases a *victory*) constantly intruding to
disturb at least our historic anticipations of the
immediate advent of the age of milk-and-water
disarmament. George III., George II., George I.,
Anne, William and Mary, James II., Charles II.,
and Oliver Cromwell, with the anterior *et ceteras*,
it is more or less *war*, not peace. But from 1815

we have grown wiser—at least, we are told so; and surely the *Times* ought to know. Perhaps; and perhaps, also, the long peace was only the period of exhaustion after a long contest—a good rest after the battle, before the combatants were ready and willing to take another turn at the sword. So long as there are separate nations all struggling to be foremost, there must be war. War is the fight for the championship of the world, and each new generation would like to try its fortune in the ring. Britain won the championship in the great wars of Napoleon I.; and, if history tells a true tale of the past, and reveals a presumption of the future, she will not be long without a hostile challenge. At all events, she will be none the worse for a little preparation in case of accidents.

It might even be possible to extract from history some horoscope of the future. History runs in cycles alternating with peace and war. The presumption, therefore, is, that the long ·quiescence which has passed away was the full cycle of an unusually long peace, and that now, once more, the war-planet is in the ascendant—ruddy Mars with the thirsty sword. The state of Europe would at least indicate something much more akin to fiery strife than to pacific disarmament. What is Italy? An exasperated slave, vowing vengeance and murder, and only awaiting the opportunity. What is Germany? A great coof, or blundering schoolboy calf, wanting to be a man, and not yet able to dare the

venture. What is Russia? A famed provincial
athlete, of monstrous size, come to the capital of
the world to make an athlete's renown. What is
France? A professional gladiator out of work,
and looking round for a new encounter. What is
Britain? The champion who has the belt, and
must be ready for all comers; a little sickly at the
present moment, and therefore likely to be called on
to enter the arena or to resign. Pah! it makes one
sick to think of politics—and of bloodshed to please
ambition. The people will be wiser some day, and
may God send them wisdom soon!

And now, then, for our rifle clubs. No doubt we
are badly off for men when the *Times* tells us that
we should arm the shopboys and men milliners and
women's tailors, and the airy-wavy-motioning rib-
bon-sellers. So we should, but not in the way the
Times tells us. We could scarcely expect them to
leave their "comfortable situations" to be whittled
into shavings by sepoy tulwars, or chopped up into
sausage meat by Hindoos and Mahommedans almost
as enervated as themselves. A joke is very well in
its way; but to ask "spruce young men," whose idea
of a sepoy has been derived principally from a black
doll, to face the genuine living article, with his
dark face and his white eyes, and a real sword in
his hand, is a stretch of imagination that surpasses
the legitimate liberty which ought to be taken
with the knights of the ladies' counter and the
cloth-yard. That is not the place to find the *army*;

but they might be made of use at home in another way.

What says the *Times* to the universal practice of the *rifle?* *There* is where our national strength ought to be developed, and where the genuine safety of the country could be most easily secured—barring one exception, which, alas! is now perhaps too late; namely, the rearing of the army in the Highlands of Scotland, where the physical circumstances of race, country, climate, and game, are superior to anything in the known world for infantry-rearing purposes. To the Highlands, however, we shall come presently : let us first dispose of our riflemen.

There are two countries that are almost invincible for defence—the United States of America and the Republic of Switzerland. If an army of a million of men were landed at New York they would make no very serious impression on the American nation. They might burn the towns and destroy the ports. They might destroy the standing material of the country, but the nation of living men they most assuredly would not subdue. In fact, they would be shot off at a calculable rate per diem, and a tole· rable guess might be made (and the Yankees would bet largely on the event) as to how long they would last. And wherefore? Because *rifle-shooting* is the great national sport; and because the revolver would help the rifle. It is the same in Switzerland. The Prussians knew better than to go into Switzerland. Puff! puff! the blue smoke would have been puffing everywhere, and all day, from behind every rock and river; and every visible Prussian would have been puffed off with a rifle plug in his brisket. A nation that takes thoroughly to the Rifle is impregnable; and what is more, the two nations that have taken most to the Rifle—the United States and Switzerland—are, curiously enough, the very two nations that have the least of human bloodshed to answer for. Monarchies that have standing armies shed blood wholesale; but Republics that practise the Rifle shed little or none at all, except in self-defence, and that is a duty, not a crime.

Instead, then, of Captain Bobadil and Baron Munchausen being the originators of the plan for defending the country at a very small cost, we can point to two countries where the thing is done. And besides, the general use of the Rifle would save the expense of the Militia—a useless force, except to furnish recruits to the army, and one that only teaches the people bad habits, drunken idleness, and debauchery: as a militia major said, " My principal duties are to protect the townspeople of L——— against my drunken militiamen." Having had the honour to be captain of a rifle-club, and having seen how the club system could be made to work, I shall venture to offer a few observations on the subject.

First. The English and the Scottish people are a warlike and weapon-loving people, and they would take enthusiastically to the Rifle if the thing were properly encouraged. The game laws more than anything else have compelled the people of this country to give up the use of fire-arms, and if ever we are invaded the game laws will be the true cause.

But the Rifle is not obnoxious to the charge of poaching, and consequently the game laws need not be jealous of its use. The Irish, it is true, might occasionally shoot a landlord with the Rifle, but they would not shoot the game; so that the landlords need not trouble themselves on the score of the Rifle.

Second. There are two parties that could encourage the use of the Rifle—the government or general authorities, and the municipalities or local authorities. Both should go together, otherwise the movement would fail. The two requisites are the grant of the rifle grounds and the grant of official prizes.

Third. The first social requisite to make Britain a rifle-shooting nation is the establishment of a universal Saturday half-holiday—no more work after 12 o'clock on Saturday. The Saturday half-holiday is the best reform that has been made in the condition of the British workman; and if it were everywhere wrought out as it has been wrought out in Edinburgh, its manifold advantages would be superabundantly apparent.

Fourth. If the Saturday half-holiday were made universal (as it ought to be, for as much work is done in the five and a half days as in the six), the *time* for rifle-practice would be gained at once. The next thing is the inducement.

The inducement should be, as in America and
Switzerland—a combination of the love of the
practice itself, as an interesting exercise of skill, and
official prizes, conferring social distinction of an
appropriate kind.   It would be absurd to make a
man a lord or a bishop because he was a good rifle-
shot—quite as absurd as to give a great scholar a
war medal or a prize revolver.   But do the thing
appropriately.   The gold medal, the silver cup, the
social honour for the rich, and the substantial
advantage for the poorer—even the prize pig for
the sturdy labourer who is rearing more young
Britons at home than he can conveniently satisfy
with bacon.   Make the Saturday afternoon a
general blaze of rifles from the Land's End to
John o' Groat's, and, if needs be, tax those who
will not attend for the prizes of those who will.
A well-armed nation is a strong nation, and a
strong nation is a safe nation, and a safe nation is
a peaceable nation.   She reposes secure in her own
strength ; and the best way to promote peace is to
arm every man who will take a pride in his
weapon and use it well.

Regarding the expense, I am thoroughly satisfied
that the average of one pound sterling, or at most
two pounds sterling per man per annum would, if
given to the clubs for prizes, yield almost any required number of skilled riflemen.   They would
receive no pay, and should find their own arms.
Thus a club of a hundred men would receive

annually one or two hundred pounds, a club of a
thousand one or two thousand pounds, and so forth.
And club would shoot against club, parish against
parish, county against county, town against town,
till the whole country would be as sharpset on the
rifle as it was once on the bow, or as it now is on
horse-racing—a sport that has done all the good it
could towards the improvement of the breed of
horses, and is now pretty much a gambling swindle,
at least Lord Derby and the Jockey Club appear to
hint as much.

If the Government would grant Rifle-Grounds
and Rifle Prizes, then there would be no lack of
Riflemen. The young would like no better amuse-
ment, and could have no better training than an
afternoon of real shooting ; not drilling and march-
ing, which are perfect nor sense for riflemen, but
" good honest shooting," as honest Roger Ascham
has it. If once trained to look steadily along the
sights, and to pull steadily with the forefinger, they
would never forget the art, and would always be
available. Military men would of course endeavour
to spoil the whole thing with the absurdities of
drill, and to make the genuine reality of good
shooting subservient to the professional ideas of
form, which are essential in an army, but useless for
rifle volunteers. All the drill that volunteer riflemen would require would be the bugle call of
" advance "—" open fire "—" cease firing "—" re-
tire :" and let every man find his own shelter and

look out for himself. If a sportsman can stalk a stag he could stalk a sentry; and if the American hunters can pull down a herd of buffaloes, our own hunters could soon pull down a regiment of any cavalry in the world, especially in a country like England, filled as it is with hedgerows and shelter of all kinds. All that is requisite is to start the principle *officially*, to give the grounds, and to advertise the prizes. Two or three hundred thousand names would be down in a month, and two or three hundred thousand trained rifle-shooters would make a fearful hole in the best army that the continent of Europe could muster. A hundred and ten years have elapsed since blood was drawn by hostile conflict on British soil; and as no other nation in the world can say as much, perhaps, we should not presume too far on the long immunity and neglect to provide for contingencies, which, however unexpected they may be, belong at least to the more ordinary current of the world's affairs. And even if the evil day should never come, there is no better recreation than rifle-shooting for a manly people. It would promote good fellowship among all classes, and make all believe that they belonged to the same country, and were doing something for it. But if the evil day *should* come, why then two or three hundred thousand *Rifles* would be admirably well employed in setting things to rights.

A WORD ON THE HIGHLANDERS.

WHERE OUR INFANTRY OUGHT TO BE RAISED.

IF ever there was a period when an investigation into the condition of the Highlands of Scotland was imperatively called for, it is at present, when Britain summons her youth to the service of their country, and when the call of patriotism might sound in vain through those northern regions which once furnished to the British army so many of its best and bravest men. The gathering cry of war is there without response—the bugle may be blown, but there is no reply, save its own empty echo—the fiery cross may pass from hill to hill, and from glen to glen, and meet only solitude and desolation, the deer browsing in an uninhabited waste, and the sheep cropping on the moss-grown hearth of some ruin that once held a household—the loudest blast that ever called men to arms would pass unheeded or unknown—no manly heart will bound, as in other times, to the trumpet-tongue of war—no nimble foot will rush to the trysting-place of honour—no broad chest will buckle on its belt in the ardour of resolution—no muscular arm will grasp the hilt and swing the whistling blade in anticipation of the well-fought field. For military purposes, the Highlands of Scotland are depopulated, and the Highlandmen are no more. The fighting men are gone, and those who remain, gathered into wretched sea-shore villages and filthy fishing-stations, though they may represent in delusive statistics the numbers of a former generation, can never supply the place of the brawny limbs and the fearless hearts that wrote the name of Scotland imperishably in the memory of Britain's foes.*

In the minds of most Scotsmen a quiet belief has settled down that the Highland population is ruined beyond recovery, and that the sooner the great landlords make short work of the remnant that remains the more merciful will be the opera-

---

* The natives of the Scottish Highlands have the two great requisites of first-rate infantry—*weight* and *wind* ; they have weight which gives them power, and wind which gives them velocity and endurance. Plenty of regiments may vie with them in courage, but none can equal them in capacity of lung and activity of limb. Wherever they appear in service we are sure to hear something remarkable about them. Even in India they are telling the same old story. "The natives all over the country are in a great fright of the 78th Highlanders, who committed such havoc at Cawnpore on the murderers there. They say that a new sort of people have come among them, fighting in petticoats, and that when they come near, sweet music issues from their bodies—that each one of these people is equal to one hundred men—that nothing can hurt them—and that they surpass even Rostum (one of the native heroes) himself."

tion. Scenes have there been presented which remind one rather of the horrors of war carried on by a barbarous people than of the even administration of law in a civilised country; and England, now that she wants an army, may pause a little, perhaps, to reflect on the true nature of the Highland clearings—so deeply injurious as those clearings have been to the martial strength of the United Kingdom. It may or it may not be true, that for private purposes a landlord may do what he likes with his own. When, however, clearings and evictions are no longer mere matters of isolated occurrence, but, extending over large districts of country, and sweeping away whole tribes of people, they rob the Queen of her men and soldiers, it may safely be contended that those clearings are no longer matters of private right, but of public concern, and that they should come under the cognisance of the State, the Parliament, the Government, and the Crown. Let the English nation and the British Parliament seriously consider this subject. Let an inquiry be instituted regarding the number of troops that on former occasions were raised in the Highland districts, and let the country be correctly informed whether Britain, in her military strength, has or has not suffered by this Highland expatriation. Let us know why, when Canada was in insurrection, nine hundred McDonalds stepped forth to do their duty as British subjects, and why, during the Crimean war, the Isle of Skye, famous

E

for its soldiers, could not even raise a militia. If
it be necessary for the country to maintain a large
army, let the country ascertain where the men are
to come from; and why it is, that in the finest
nursery for infantry soldiers that any nation could
desire, there should scarcely be a recruit, much less
the invincible regiments that formerly came forth
at the nation's bidding. England, not less than
Scotland, is concerned; and perhaps the present
crisis in our military affairs may not be allowed to
pass away without an intelligent inquiry into circumstances that have no parallel in the history of
any other civilised country.

Let us hear what a Highlander has said on this
subject. " The county of Sutherland, where I was
born and brought up, is almost exclusively the
property of the Duke of Sutherland and his anti-
slavery Duchess. In this Highland county alone
you can set a compass, with twenty-five miles of a
radius,. but within the circumference you will not
find one hundred acres which have been cultivated
for the last twenty-seven years; and I recollect
when two thousand able-bodied young men could
be raised in the same circuit in twenty-four hours.
I have seen myself about five hundred dwelling-
houses on that estate all in flames at once." That
is the meaning of Highland depopulation, and that
is the system that has deprived the country of its
soldiers. The repulse from the Redan was the
moral of this story; and the disgrace of the British

arms in the presence of French success on the never-to-be-forgotten 8th of September, 1855, may perhaps be a warning for the future guidance of the country. In the history of Great Britain it would have been a good investment to have brought from Canada as many Highlanders as would have taken the Redan, even though the royal yacht should have been sent on purpose to bring them over.

It is a grand thing for a nation to have good infantry—five feet ten in height—forty inches round the chest—twenty inches round the calf of the leg—who can march fifty miles a day—can climb mountains—cross rivers—bivouac in the snow—live on anything—as hard as oaks—as swift as deer—as strong as bulls—as brave as lions—incomparable at a rush—capital shots—steady in camp—unsurpassed in the field—with the proud heritage of an invincible name—who, only let them go, and the proudest of the foes of Britain would recoil before the hurricane of steel. Such men may be only Scottish Highlanders, but there *were* such men, and fifty thousand of them were raised for the Peninsular war. It is a grand thing to have good infantry; for all great battles, and all great wars, depend ultimately on the conduct of the infantry. It is impossible to overestimate their value. The destinies of empires hang upon their resolution; the fate of nations is staked upon their fortitude; the progress of the world itself is borne onward on the point of their bayonets. Something more imposing there may be in the tramp of cavalry, but there the war-horse is copartner with the man; or in the thunder of artillery, but there the unconscious instrument is the death-dealer to the foe; or in the giant ship with her tier upon tier of cannon, but the ship bears all onward alike into the midst of the stormy fray. In infantry alone does the soldier stand forward in his unaided manhood; he trusts neither to his horse, nor to his cannon, nor to his ship, but to himself. It is he and death in the duel of their single combat; the spirit of man looking through the veil of nature on the immortal vision of honour. The destinies of the world depend on the conduct of its infantry. One infantry regiment that will never flinch from the face of mortal, and will charge successfully any similar number of any foe that can be brought before it, is a jewel in the diadem of the greatest monarch that ever did or ever can exist on the face of the earth. The country that can grow the best infantry is the foremost country in the world. All the wealth of the world cannot produce them. Every such invincible man is a thing of worth like a Koh-i-noor. There *were* Highlanders of that same mark, and they have been hounded out of their homes and banished like unprofitable wretches; shipped off to Canada in a heap, at the cheapest rate—done " at the lowest figure;" so poor in the famine times that they could not pay for themselves; so worthless in the eyes of aristocracy that the Government

combined with the landlords to " get rid of them."
Yet worthless as they were, they are in the solemn
times of war worth more than all military mechanics; worth more than ships, horses, guns, or
fortifications; worth more than all else whatever;
worth more than the Bank of England and all the
wealth of all the aristocracy landed or commercial.
They are worth the one thing that valour alone
can preserve—the sacred honour of their native
country.

Time will show whether Britain may ever again
require to stand on her defence; but certain it is
that the best, the cheapest, and the most profitable
way to grow an army, would be to grow it in the
Highlands of Scotland, even if the depopulated
lands were hired on purpose.

SHOOTING.

THE accompanying diagram represents the ordinary kind of good shooting that ought to be made with a revolver at twenty-five paces. The space within the lines represents a sheet of foolscap paper opened out—16 inches in height and 12¾ inches in breadth. This shooting must not be taken as the best that can be made, but as a fair specimen of ordinary good shooting that can be made by a good shot at any time with a pistol taken out of store.

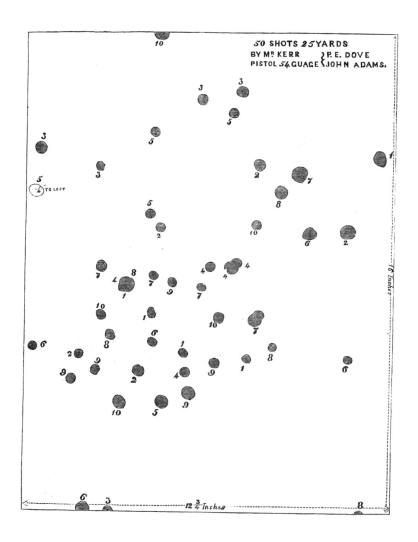

50 SHOTS 25 YARDS
BY Mr KERR } P. E. DOVE
PISTOL 54 GUAGE } JOHN ADAMS.

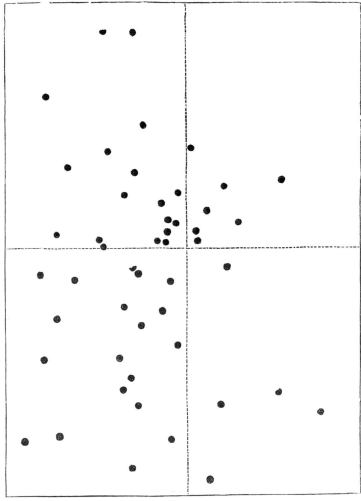

Fifty shots, at 25 paces, by Mr. John Adams. Size—same as Diagram of
Mr. Kerr's shots.

A WORD TO THE WISE.

DEFENCE OF THE COLONIES.—IMPORTANT CIRCULAR.

THE following "Circular Despatch" has been issued from the Colonial Office to the Governors of Colonies:—

" SIR,—I am desirous that you should take every opportunity of impressing upon your government that it behoves them not to neglect that reasonable amount of warlike preparation during peace which it is desirable should be everywhere maintained.

" It is obvious that the state of defence in which each colony is maintained must have a great influence upon the general resources of the empire during war.

" They will be a source of weakness in so far as it is necessary for the land and sea forces of the mother country to defend them against aggression, and a source of strength if while they are able to repel any ordinary efforts of an enemy's squadron, they will afford shelter and support to our own forces.

" In fact, the defences of the colonies, from whatever source maintained, form parts of the defences of the empire, and it will be necessary that the Secretary of State for War should have on record information as to the state of defence in which each colony is kept.

" I would, therefore, suggest that you should once a year call upon the officer commanding Her Majesty's troops in   , to report to you upon the numbers and state of any local forces maintained by the colony—whether permanently embodied or as militia or volunteers—pointing out how often they meet for drill, and as far as he can judge their state of discipline and military efficiency. The officer commanding Her Majesty's troops will add to this report the report of the commanding officer of artillery upon the numbers and efficiency of all guns, carriages, platforms, and military stores (if any) under the care of the colonial government, and the report of the commanding officer of Royal Engineers upon the condition of all fortifications, batteries, barracks, magazines, tanks, or other military structures (if any), the maintenance of which has been intrusted to the colonial government.

" I have to add that corresponding instructions will be sent to the officer commanding the troops in

" I have, &c.,

" H. LABOUCHERE."